BEAUTY OF COLORS

Poems

By

Cleanne Lynn Johnson

ISBN: 978-1-7923-6116-6

TABLE OF CONTENTS

ABOUT THE BOOK

These poems will lift your inner spirit, and transform your life, give you a sense of purpose, belonging an appreciation for beauty in and around you. This collection of poems will draw you to the core of the earth and make you realize you are special, unique and created by a creator being one with the earth. So, fuel yourself from these poems an arise to the top.

Forever you

As mysterious as the depth of the earth
As polish as charcoal cream, eyes as bright and shiny as the farthest star in the galaxy,
With voice as soft as jellyfish, swimming in the abyss of the ocean floors.
Hair is thick, black and curly, with its pattern as a raw amethyst in its natural form.
She looks lost in her thoughts, lost in whom she is,
Lost in who she was created to be.
Is this darkness a curse? Is it a shame to look upon?
Like some forbidden fruit locked away in the Garden of Eden.
The light has shone as darkness and it has become a sapphire.
Radiating in the atmosphere, blinding the eyes that dare glimpsed at its majestic form,
Not wanting to be recognized,
Her swarthiness took the breath of her passerby.
But she bent her head in dismay, not knowing her beauty
Her only thought was her darkness
If only she knew…
Her color was her strength! Her darkness was her majesty!
Her color was who she is! Who she was always meant to be!

Ashamed

Strands of thick, wavy, curly hair that thrives from its roots upwards
Brush through the street day and night.
It is crowded with Queens not looking at each other's curls as an epitome of Black Womanhood,
Instead, they're on strands of long, straight hair that is deemed as what is good and socially acceptable.
WHAT IS SOCIALLY ACCEPTABLE?
The streets are crowded day and night with Queens gazing on wishful thinking,
Dreaming of the day when the strands of curly beauty will be transformed too straight and manageable.
Waiting a lifetime until the expiration date
Until the clock strikes no more, instead of treasuring,
Instead of embracing each coil like a complicated treasure map,
Leading to an eternity of bliss.
Strands of thick, wavy, curly hair.
It is vast! Beyond comparison
Styling, braiding, and twisting curly strands.
Making it rise above the other strands on the street that dare to compete.

Magic unfolds

Black as the crevice of the mountains on the brightest light of dusk
Eyes as white as snow, gazing into the wonders of the crystal ball
Like the future was unfold and everything was naked, vulnerability at its best
Staring intensely, trying to decipher what secret lies beneath the surface,
Searching the soul inside out for something.
Something magical that would save her from herself.
A voice whispering, have you found your destiny child?
Look beyond the image in the ball.
What do you see my child?
Tell me, what do you see?
Did you come across creeping nightmares with shadows in the dark?
Look deeper!
Look at the blackness of your earth and everything within it
Rip the layers of self-inflicted hate that overtook every love for blackness
Behold! The beauty found in your skin.

Reflection of Greatness

Light shines on the black emerald without reproach,
Bouncing off the creek of its four corners and reflects in the mirror.
Radiance as bright as the sun itself
Not wanting to know the emerald's past, it's becoming a phase.
Looking for the reflection to show the streams of its never-ending nudity.
The whiteness that each curve displays
The aliveness of the elegantly in sync twists
Its brown, chocolate luminosity even the light.
Waiting for years, for that emerald
Not realizing, metamorphosis of that rare diamond
Not asking questions, but patiently waiting for self-acceptance,
In the period where emerald is the embodiment of extra ordinary kings and queens.

Photo by: Author

Love Me Back

Why do you feel the need for lighter skin my love?
When the sun reflects on its majesty, glowing on its melanin
Causing an infusion of exquisiteness.
Lighter skin,
What is its purpose?
Why do you feel the need for validation?
Bleaching out thick layers of beauty, just wanting to see the epidermis.
Living in regret, convinced the creator did you some injustice by making you who you are.
The spots of unevenness, the bumps under the ridges of the knuckles.
Looking at the face and cannot decide its true nature
Its true beauty in its rawest form.
What is seen in the light, the sun shines upon?
Bleached layers day after day,
My melanin is crying,
Wanting to come back home
Screaming!
What have you done to me?
Why are you so cruel to the gift that I have given you?
Why are you so ashamed of me?

Am I not the soil of the earth?
Maker and ruler of all beings?
My beauty is within you!
I am all around you, so please love me the way that I love you
Give me life, the way I have given it to you.
Please take me back, do not let them make you think that I was your mistake
let me glow in my thick melanin dermis.

Masks

Broken in his own sweat.
Self-love takes strength and perseverance,
The ability to be enchanted with the flaws in the mirror.
Beaten down by the expectations of masculinity that society has forced on his shoulders.
Yearning to break through the drops of his heavy burden and pain that he gracefully carried over the years.
Looking at his reflection he can also see a creature of no value,
One who has suffered a great loss only wanting better
But the pieces of body parts in his shattered mirror have been distributed,
Through the north, south, east and west.
Wanting to identify with his ancestor, but fear of knowing, fear of the realization of self,
He rejects his very essence, but inside his soul is talking,
Desiring for the facade to be over
His ancestor's voices, words, and actions can be seen in his behavior and mannerism,
He is fighting a battle that only he can resolve.

Little Leaf

Leaves floating in the atmosphere
Embracing the breeze through its tiny pores
Not sure where to place its mark in the world.
Have I been here before?
Have I seen this before?
On the horizon, the wind keeps brushing me
Wandering me through its tides
To land on an object, I do not wish to be part of
I want to float in the air
To continue to dance, twisting and twirling in the unison of its breeze
For years upon years, to find myself
To land on the homeland where I belong
To change my colors, shed my skin
Turn yellow, orange, green, brown or black,
Not conforming to the destiny of other leaves
So, I fly…
Flying away from birds, wanting to snap me and lay me to the ground
To be sit upon, spit upon, with its feces on my beloved body.
Passerby's looking turning their noses at my condition, saying,
"This leaf has allowed the birds and wind to dampen her spirit and crush her."

Seasons

Green or red apples? Both.
All blossoming together on the same tree embedded with roots that tame its stems.
Cut inside reviles layers upon layers, until the soul is exposed for all to see
Discovered that in the middle, the main substance lies there
Waiting to be touched by deserving hands
The main substances lie there.
Evolving and nurturing the apple to be nutritious with just one bite
Desirable for the lucky eyes that pays attention to its outer skin
Tempting, almost irresistible to the body's craving.
It takes a season, for the apple to mature into its prime.
Thriving at its time, at the right temperature.
If it came in winter, the soul would die,
If it were picked prematurely, it would not be enjoyed to its fullest potential.
It knows the time of its abundance
It does not worry what color it is; it just simply wants to be an apple
Blooming amongst other apples
Sharing its stages, sharing its stories to the other apples
Waiting for the special someone to examine and say,
"You are gorgeous, and your soul will be planted."

Photo by: Author

Canvas of Colors

Colors of earth in the rainbow
Cannot be separated, or smeared
Celestially connected with each other creating a canvas of euphoria
Yet so different in their own singularity.
Every pigment, every ray emission has its own unique purpose.
Its reason for being what it is, what it is supposed to do?
There are no inferior or superior, no argument.
Cohabiting together
To craft regality in its own unique form in the sky where they survive
And others being on the galaxy marvel in awe
Curious as to where its creativity lies.
Wondering why earth is not like the rainbow
They are created equal, no flaws, no wickedness was found on their color,
Until the darker rainbow thought that the bright rainbow gave out more luminosity and glow.

Tell Me Why

Under the ray of the hot sun
Face sweating,
Mind racing
Waiting to see the kingdom come
Why do you subject yourselves to this?
Why do you tolerate such torture?
Haven't you suffered enough?
Haven't your bones been broken to its extreme?
Isn't your mind tired of the abuse?
Isn't your body exhausted?
In the past, you were look upon as the "IT"
The fashion, the in style
People all over the planet want to have a piece of you
Crave for your presence by their side.
You could go anywhere and be treated with respect
With the dignity and favor that you know you deserve
So why do you subject yourselves to hot sun?

Save Me

Weather roaming and complaining
I need to be heard.
I need my voice to be harkened to by the invaders
That succumbed to making my home unrecognizable.
What is being done to my home?
The place of plenty, the breath of substantive.
Why are men cutting down my breath?
Stealing the essence of what makes me feel special
What makes me, me?
Why is the earth crying for help?
Taking through the cracks the very life it values
The sea is talking, but no one is listening
No one is listening to its weeps to be complete again
The winds are whispering, but everyone seem to close the doors
Shutting out their ears to its agony, blind eye at its best.
Summer is fighting with fall to take its place,
Winter continues to double in the fall and spring
I am upset, because I am not valued, and now I shake my
Garment, I kneel down, shouting, fighting the urge to surrender
That is enough!
Come to your senses and see that the only person you are damaging, Is me.

Unknowingness

The trees are blowing bliss with raindrops
Crawling on the green spine of the leaves
As it slides its way through, craving to be one with the earth
There is serenity in accepting its purpose
Dropping to the floor as its children splashes on the blackness of the soil.
Inhale,
Exhale,
Embracing…
Life is blossoming inside the womb, as well as pain is beginning to form
Unaware…
Is it beauty?
Or the opposite?
The child awaits, a surrounding of sadness and happiness and one
In between, there are children,
Eating red clay, rolling in the mud to fall asleep
While stomach is roaring like thunder on a dark night
And the hunger pains keep electrifying
With so much food waste,
The populations are gasping for air
And abundance of food, not in the mouths,
Of those who need it the most.

Photo by: Author

Dear Momma

Mother you have sacrificed everything for me.
Introducing me into the world was a difficult task for you,
Yet still you labored for nine months in agony just to keep me safe.
You brushed through the dark woods overwhelmed with despair,
Chopped every tree in your path that would have led to my destruction
And combed the cobwebs on the roads,
Giving me a vivid vision to my journey.
For this, I will forever extend my gratitude towards you.
You had no excuses, no justifications to why not.
I was as a flower and you were my keeper
Feeding me with fertilizer to enrich my soul
Watering my mind with your words of wisdom
Plucking out every weed that would have seek to devour my flesh
It was unquestionable, you just wanting the best for me
You wanted to see me flourish into what I was created to be
When you went to bed drenched in your tears
Eyes swollen as your pillow absorbed all the frustration of motherhood

You would never let your flower see your daily struggles, to see the light at the end of your tunnel.
Sometimes you forget to cry, even when the sorrow encamped around you
That is how strong as a rock you are,
You are not easily broken!
Superhuman at its best…
Your life has become a mountain of joy
Even though you think back of the past
The height of the mountain you overcame, enveloped and crashed the agony that
Was inflicted in you when I was a child.

Hello Nature

The river continues to flow down creating a symphony of harmony
In the steep valley where the mountains were so elevated, it could not be seen.
Clouds coalesce in the heaven sky,
Shape shifting its way to paradise to anyone who paid attention.
Echoes of duck conversations,
As they swam in unison splashing in the water quacking in joy.
While the huge rat made its nest, finding its home in the rocks adjacent to the river.
The river…
The river was a habitat too many who swam
Salmons are in its glory, visibly swimming upstream to say fair well
To the life of the sea, entering the life they had waited for.
Nothing could be compared to this
No place could be compared to this
The trees are whispering songs of the singing birds
While the eagles are gliding as the gusty winds sizzles through their feathers.
Looking for the perfect prey.
Human beings are engaging in daily conversations,

While nature seems to be going along fine, not deviating from its plan.

Work So Hard

Why do we work so hard?
Sweat falling through the glands of our pigmented skin
Breaking backs, painful joints from all the tireless 24/7
Bruised fingers, carpel tunnel
And we still don't enjoy the fruits of our labor.
Monday to Friday, Sunday to Saturday
No day of rest, no tune with family
Neglecting their smiles while enjoying the Sunday specials.
Why do we work so hard?
To be like the Joneses or to be better than the Joneses?
Why can't we be comfortable with what we have?
What we have achieved?
Do you find satisfaction sweating miserably without enjoying the fruits of your labor?
Without being joyful of the little things?
Do the little things matter to us?
Shirking our earthly duties and wanting more money in the bank, a bigger house, a faster car
That we will not enjoy.
We believe that we will live forever.
NEVER!
We all have an expiration date
So please tell me,
Why do we work so hard?

Little Black Bird

I look at the black bird
And see my reflection, as if somehow it was I.
Unconcerned, head held high,
Soaring with self-assurance looking for food.
On an epic journey, to be the best black bird known in the heavens,
Look at the black bird
Hovering over its creation
Definite that its black baby birds will conquer the skies just as she has.
Never falling short to their needs
Feeding them so passionately, fortitude complete.
Momma birdy in love.
Will the other birds be chirping?
Jealous of the black bird's nobility?
But they are black, why do they care so much about these black birds?
The mother bird looks around,
Chirping back nonchalantly
Her little black birds are the future of
The heavens, their fight will be visible throughout the skies,
It is easy to recognize and show adulation to the one that it has created.

Photo by: Author

Liberation

Freedom is dark
It has always been for the oppressed
Those whose voices were never appreciated.
Waiting, watching for the darkness of night to be hailed
When would darkness be free?
Liberated from the chains of its eternal bondage
Definitely not in the daylight!
It will never be seen in the brightness of day
Matching the stairs of famous buildings,
Head lifted, proud bloated
Has the day finely come for the voices of my people to be acknowledged?
Or will that time never exist
Will we forever be enslaved by the suffocation of the daylight?
Sitting on the porch dismayed in defeat,
Listening to the verdict of the brutal killing of our dark men and women.
Seeking justice, for an entire race that is too rare to be extinct,
The melanin is too rich to be put to waste
It is too creamy and pure to vanish into the abyss
GOD FORBID!
We keep on fighting though progress is slow
But the time will come
Freedom will be disguised as the new slavery for all.

Essence of Life

Life is more than skin color
It is more than being red or yellow, black or white
It is about love, the purest thing a human could ever experience.
Life is about looking beyond one's physical appearance
And seeing the authenticity of their heart.
It is about respect.
Seeing more than just a pigment
Searching the soul,
Yet not trusting everyone
Because of pigment similarities.
Life is about observing character,
Monitoring the habits of people
Watching someone by their deeds,
Like a snake focusing on its prey every move.

Experiencing This Bliss

Walking the beach basking in the rising heat of the sun
The rays glowing on her ebony skin tone
Making her as twice as radiant as she was before.
The bees are buzzing, on the coconut trees
Looking for nectar to feed on
Ripe mangoes are falling like leaves, being in communion with the land.
On the beach she lay on the pink sandy shores, basking in the sun,
Absorbing the penetrating rays, apathetic of the sun darkling of the skin,
But enjoying the effect
Appreciating how the rays, hugs her body
Not thinking of people's reaction,
She is in her tanning world.

Rolling Deep

The rocks rolling down the steep mountain sides
Loose soil, detaching itself from home onto a foreign place
Tumbling, bumbling down, body no longer one big ball
But not broken into large pieces
At the bottom of the precipice.
The river life is in abundance.
Bus people are in fear of the unknown
Shaking, like an earthquake to the rock's mystery,
A baby is in the arms of man, innocently sleeping
Heedless to the danger
It takes two days, to get to the village.
Night of darkness in the deep mountains
Life is not that easy, explosion of rocks to give way to new roads,
People seeking for a better place.

Photo by: Author

Beautiful Skin

Dark skin why are you amounted with so much sorrow?
Why do you suffer so much in silence?
No one being able to hear your SOS
Why do you bow your head in agonizing shame?
Self-sabotaging your youth, neglecting your happiness
For the sake of others to feel a sense of comfortability.
Why are you hated for who you are?
For the color of your skin?
Oh, little do they know
They are ignorant to the fact that you are the soul of the earth,
The very thing the keeps hearts alive.
The mother of all human beings, creator of all there is
Unique from the foundation of the earth,
You were molded in the shape of an exquisite sculpture,
Too priceless to be bought with a price
It cannot be replaced.
Your beauty is evidence of your destination
Appreciate your deep beauty my love
Appreciate the uniqueness in your pigmentation
Life is full of surprises and you are not a mistake,
You are the inheritance of the earth.

Not an Easy Road

The pain in her eyes can be seen a mile away,
Woe had always been her portion
As she watched her daughter across the savannah desserts,
Fighting the elements thrown at her
Chasing off the lions,
Stoning the elephants and other wild animals that were after her sanity.
Her body is slender as the sticks are on her back,
Struggling to carry them in an upright position
She walks fast in the abyss, inhaling the scent of brimstone that surrounded her
Not wanting to fall on the red soil
And stain her white dress, spoiling its virginity.
She trod along the treacherous, narrow path
With blood in her hands, fear in her eyes
As she placed one foot in front each other
Not wanting to succumb to the pressure.
Her narrow path guided her to the nearest house
Fading away in the distance, her tears rolled down her checks into her mouth
When will I see her again?

The Death of Me

He looked at her heavenly.
Dumbfounded at the beauty that beheld him,
Staring at what seemed like stars in the pupil of her brown eyes
Glowing its way into his heart; completely mesmerized!
Wondering how did he ever get so lucky to be in the presence of such majesty?
He studied her skin, for his next science project
Awestruck at each layer that glowed in its own unique form
Counting the cells that lies within,
It was not just about the outer layers, oh no!
He marveled and caressed her hair flowing through his fingers
The black mole, looking like a starfish,
The intricate lines on her hand and feet as if it was a map,
Or even a treasure hunt leading to a destination unknown
That is filled with diamonds and gold.
Fascinated! He was about to blindly follow that path with her
Unknowingly, but certain that his toils and hardship would be worth it.
She would be worth it.
The venom that he would drink from her was as sweet as the finest wine

But that was what she was to him, his own little sweet poisonous wine
That fermented on the shelf, getting stronger as the minutes passed.
He knew the risks; he knew that if he drank it, it would be the death of him
But the irresistibility was as cocaine to a drug addict.
He could not let go of the beauty in his arms
He needed her even if she was the death of him.

Cruel, Cruel World

Dancing to the music in my ears
Watching the passersby's run for the buses and trains
Staring out a window looking at a little girl, holding the arms of her mom
She looks so innocent, like a baby just craving the love of her family
She could see her reflection in this five-year-old
Carefree, her head covered in a brown Hijab.
What is her future going to look like?
Will fear groom in her heart from people who do not know her, but only hate her because her religion is different from the norm
Is the world going to treat her like any other regular privileged child?
Is it going to call her by her name, accept all of her and her choices?
Innocent smiles with excitement in her body,
Feeling like the prettiest five-year-old
With her little hands latched on to her mother's thumb, never wanting to let go.
In her flower stitched lace dress, touching the ground,
She does not know the hate of the world on her.
Waving at everyone who smiled at her
It could be seen by how she watched people with nothing but love in her eyes.

Her culture is reflected in her attitude and behavior.
She respects and loves everyone,
Not knowing that the love she gives will be returned as hate.
I brushed my Hijab to one side and folded my hands,
As if today, I was one with that little girl.

Photo by: Author

Wrath

Life is sinking with the ground
The chaos overtook everything that was normal,
Everything that had a sense of familiarity to home.
People's villages are going down in the soil
And hopelessness was all over,
Not being able to save themselves from the wrath of Mother Nature
Rivers are becoming one with the oceans as they roar in unison
Mother Nature was angry that we exchanged centuries of abuse
When she only gave all of her.
The soil is mulchy,
Lofty and muddy from her outcries upon the land
It poured on the feet of young children
Kicking their shoes, sliding from end to end unaware of her wrath.
Mud, dripping down the mountains like hot lava, mud pools created in the north.
The poor villagers are trapped in the chaos of mother's madness
Not wanting to back down without a fight.
She is shouting, screaming,
Leave me pure just the way I gave myself to you.

Life is Unfair

Shame and disperse in her eyes
Not wanting to move forward
But rendered useless if she remained stagnant at where she was
Sack of cloth cover her face, hiding the shame that tried to eat her alive
Falling to her feet weeping,
Life is unfair!
The wells of water on her chest suffocating her breath
But there was nothing that could be done
The sticks for fire, was all around, burning her feet
Heels becoming as black as charcoal.
She walks the distance miles, and miles without assurance that there will be an end
But there was no point in stopping; she was already too far to give up,
So, she walks as her dress rubbed against the pieces of rocks that her garment swept,
Not wanting the bandits to see her, all too familiar to her past, she brushes through the bushes
Covering her face with a black veil counting her steps briskly
Only a few more to go
Life is unfair.

Homeland

Why have you escaped your birth land?
To go into a place of the unknown where you are not welcomed?
Where you are seen as a threat, a liability that needs to be extinct?
Mass genocide
Do you remember the triumph of your people?
The drums, rich culture embedded in their spirit.
The music that kept your heart beating with undulating waves of calmness.
Can you see the land that left its imprint upon your thigh, neck and arms?
Are you free, from everything?
The distance that seemed far away, but only a mile of pain and suffering.
Do you think of the day, when all this will be over, and you will return to the soil?

Hey Skin

Skin you are beautiful from the top of your head to the sole of your feet.
You illuminate with a gloss that cannot be compared
The sun, moon and stars shine upon your glow,
Giving an essence of belonging and acceptance.
The way you made one feel when their fingers trace the lines of your tiger marks
These smooth lines that kindly define your elasticity,
The density of the weight, the power of dominance that you project.
Your large surface area that you repair over and over.
Being the carpenter of your own story
Not waning your characteristics that you love about yourself fade away.
The difference, colors, textures and firmness.
You encountered the pimples, scrapes, scars, insect bites,
But still you rise to the surface and protect like nothing even happened.

Photo by: Author

Mamma A

Africa is calling for our attention
Please listen to the voice of its wailing
Desiring to be saved from its generational torture from the Western World.
Its people are finally beginning to open their eyes
Seeing the world through a different lens
Watching it from a different perspective
Not the one portrayed, but the one neglected
Why were these lies told about our first people?
The nation where others inherited from it, everything that they own
Tricking our land into feeling inferior, when they were always
Royalty wrapped in gold,
We were taken away not knowing the land
But the sense of something that was desperately missing
Weighing on our forgotten souls, home sick is the root of the pain
Until that day when we shall return to the land of ancestral birth
And fill the world, that has encompassed and degraded us.
Standing on the throne proud of our melanin
Shouting we are black, and we are back.

Assurance

Ocean is covered with life, surrounded with species swimming with a purpose
Every creature in survival
While keeping the large body of water thriving with life.
Different species are self-aware,
Born with instinct to know their role in this vast place
Aware of the danger that compass around them,
Yet still swimming with carefree of life
Wanting to populate the beds of the oceans,
Singing hallelujah deep in the bottom pit of the beds,
Not fearing the darkness of the ocean's depth
Knowing who they are not,
No questions asked, am I a shark or a human?
Confidence of self is engrained in their DNA,
From birth, not fearing the oceans,
Not asking, could you teach me to swim or breathe under the oceans?

Complete in the Sky

Laying on the sand looking into the sky,
Marveling how nature resembled the essence of what life is supposed to be.
Laying on the sand looking into the sky,
Seeing the togetherness of white clouds
As they move in unison to the luminescence of the sun
Working together, thriving together in the atmosphere's current
Laying, feeling the finest of sand on my skin
Envisioning myself floating on the clouds.
The clouds did not see that something was upon them.
Bewilderment as its finest.
What was upon them looked nothing like their white fluffiness
Nor their lengthy surface.
A foreigner in need of some place to call home.
Laying in the sand looking into the sky
Astonished at how they embraced that forcing object
One who looked different on the outside, but identical on the inside
Making it part of their whiteness.
Not complaining of its darkness overshadowing their destination,
But the dark cloud began to shine making them complete.
No discrimination, no prejudice in the blue sky.

My Womb

Eyes open to the world full of opportunities at the tip of her finger
But for crying aloud which one is she going to receive
Is she predestined even before she was molded and made in the womb of her mother?
Who desperately needed a child?
Or was she made out of love?
So many questions, so little answers, but one thing is certain
She is beautiful.
Her hands are soft, but her eyes contain so much pain from her mother
Her warm drips ran through her face while closing her moon shape eyes in sleep.
Dreaming of the purpose, all the whys that kept her in wonderland
The life that will be coming at her with force
And vague, moaning that made her felt that she was in a comfortable place
Between her mother's bosom,
Moping for protection for the rest of her life
Not wanting this moment to rush by,
Not wanting to be responsible for her actions,
When she opens her eyes,

It is night and she realized that she had children of her own to feed and clothe.

Photo by: Author

Imagination

She sat at the lunch table and their eyes interlocked with each other,
Piecing at her very soul, sending chills all over her body.
Why is he looking in her direction?
Why does he feel the need to stare?
What does he want?
These thoughts began to cluster her mind as her sense of reasoning vanished.
I am his next victim!
Avoiding eye contact at all cost, tilting her head down hoping that his interest will fade away.
She could still see him looking at her,
Sweat began running down her face and back, wondering
I am the next victim!
A group of male friends came to sit with him and in a few seconds,
All eyes were on her.
The darkness of her skin becoming more uncomfortable,
Wishing she could peel off every bit of it for the sake of not being seen.
She might be the next sacrifice of their fraternity.
Her eyes became itchy, as he rushed over to her table
When he was near the table, she began to wriggle her chair to exist.
Not wanting to be a part of anything that he wanted to do

Then the warmest smile came, showing his white teeth "Hello, my name is Mike, and I couldn't stop staring at your beautiful dark skin and your lovely check bones," She was relieved, I am not a victim.

Photo by: Author

Bye-Bye Green

Trees are falling in the forest like leaves in the beginning of winter.
No one can hear the sounds of the rumbling trunks,
Beating on the marshy soil, decaying like they had never existed in the first place
Their home is gone; everything they once know is now no more.
No more visits from the wildlife,
Making a home to feed their offspring.
No creeping crawlers to sip their juices off their back,
Visualization of life being found is now a thing of the pass.
Resemblance of a bittersweet memory that has been gone with the breeze
There is no seed to replace and eventually,
Rain will cease, the air will be polluted again with the filth of human emission
But there is no remorse in their actions.
I am being destroyed she wailed!
Just as the air, as the river and oceans.
I thought I was needed for the life of every living soul,
I thought I was the essence of what living truly is
But materialistic things are worth more than breath.

Silly Little Girl

Nose was ridged, straight and pointy
Lips thin, hair straight, check bone were high above her mouth
That was her vision,
That was what she wanted to see when her reflection exhibited in the mirror.
Her hands are shaking, sweating with perfectionist anxiety
Trying to create a clay doll that looks like her,
But the images she had imbedded in her head over the years did not fit the clay dolls appearances.
She wanted so dearly to make something that looked like her,
But over the years, the beauty she saw as not her own,
She wept, no longer knowing who the creator made her to be.
The longing to have a picture-perfect image of her made her lost.
Wanting to bury the false notion of what beauty is supposed to look like,
She tries to recapture, but beauty was always supposed to be oneself.

ABOUT THE AUTHOR

Cleanne Lynn Johnson is the author of the book, Love My Colors. She started writing short stories and poetry in high school to express her feelings and found writing to be a safe haven.

She has a master's in public health, and practices as a dietitian in New York. When she isn't writing short stories and poetry, she enjoys cooking, hiking, reading, sewing and encouraging people from all different nationality, culture and ethnicities that they are special, unique and beautiful. Find more about Cleanne Lynn Johnson at her website https://youarespecial.info or on

Facebook: https://www.facebook.com/beautyofcolors66/

Pinterest: https://www.pinterest.com/beautyofcolors66/

MORE FROM CLEANNE LYNN JOHNSON

This book is for all those people – especially young girls who have been belittled and made fun of, just based on their skin color.

Diversity is beautiful, and every skin-color matters – be it black, olive, brown, or white. Natashia learns to be content in her own skin, with time and a few lessons on the way. Yes, she may be darker skinned than her mother and the rest of the residents at the island. Yes, she may also be darker-skinned than her lighter-skinned father and the rest of the kids at school… but she is her own person – whatever her skin-color.

www.ingramcontent.com/pod-product-compliance
Ingram Content Group UK Ltd.
Pitfield, Milton Keynes, MK11 3LW, UK
UKHW020137250726
13967UKWH00002B/718

9 781792 361166